PRAISE FOR REFLECT

This is a book to use every day, but especially on those days when you need help with changing your outlook on life and your relationships. Each section begins with a poetic reflection, followed by three ways to investigate that reflection in your life. You are inspired to be present with each sensation, person, and event in your life, and to let go of what blocks the joy and satisfaction that Presence can reveal. My personal favorite is, "What is one worry you could release with the next out-breath?"

—Jan Chozen Bays, MD and Zen Roshi,
author of *Mindful Eating*

This book is a masterpiece. It is bound to become a classic for those of us who are serious about the business of true awakening. It is also a breath of fresh air. Donald Altman knows how to formulate the deepest wisdom with such an easy, tender and compassionate touch. And a wildly funny remark is never far away! I love this book already and know that it will inspire me for years to come. With tremendous craft Altman is able to awake the reader to the brilliancy of this moment. As he puts it, *"The mind is like a wild mustang that will kick you unless trained."* This is the clearest, most poetic and most practical book on mindfulness I have seen in years. A lasting gift!

D1534143

Reflect skillfully combines wisdom and humor, and I found myself not only reflecting but laughing at times, which drives the point home really well! The profound insights are accessible to everyone. I loved this book.

—David Nez, artist and
author of *The Tree of Visions*

Donald's wonderful book *Reflect* offers insightful and mindful "reflections" on the most important aspects of our lives. In our relationships, we should see partners, friends, and relatives with fresh eyes. Love involves the mindful deepening to the richness and subtleties of our connectedness. We should lighten up and enjoy laughter and humor so that we can truly open up to the here and now.

—John B. Arden, PhD,
author of *Mind-Brain-Gene*

In a series of poetic aphorisms, Donald Altman caresses the topics of simplicity, peace, love, and bliss to illuminate the stuck places in our psyche and bring us home to our deeper selves. *Reflect* is truly magical.

—John Nelson, author of
A Guide to Energetic Healing

Serenity is closer than we think, no further from us than the pages of this gem of a book. Every reflection within is an opportunity for heightened awareness, an open invitation to embrace life's journey without mindless distraction, reveling in those spaces between thoughts, where we are inspired to receive the light of discovery and can reflect on the blessings of our truest, most pure and profound nature.

—Randall Fitzgerald,
author and journalist

Reflection is a process of taking stock of yourself and where you stand in the world. As simple as it may sound it takes practice to develop the habit of practicing reflection. Fortunately, Donald Altman's newest book, *Reflect*, provides insights into how you can make reflection a habit. Doing so will energize yourself as well as make you more aware of how you deliver your best to others.

—John Baldoni, author of
Grace: A Leader's Guide to a Better Us

REFLECT

Awaken to
the Wisdom
of the Here
and Now

DONALD ALTMAN

Published by:
PESI Publishing & Media
PESI, Inc.
3839 White Ave.
Eau Claire, WI 54703

Cover: Amy Rubenzer
Layout: Bookmasters & Amy Rubenzer

ISBN: 9781683732167

 PESI
Publishing & Media
pesipublishing.com

ABOUT THE AUTHOR

◆

Donald Altman, MA, LPC, is a psychotherapist, award-winning author, and former Buddhist monk. Featured in *The Mindfulness Movie* and profiled in the *Living Spiritual Teachers Project*, he has written over 15 books that teach how to incorporate mindfulness into daily life. Award-winning books include: *The Mindfulness Toolbox*—winner of two Gold IBPA Benjamin Franklin™ Awards as best book in the "Psychology" and "Body-Mind-Spirit" categories, *Clearing Emotional Clutter*—selected "One of the Best Spiritual Books of 2016" and *The Mindfulness Code*—chosen "One of the Best Spiritual Books of 2010."

Donald has reached out to the community by serving as vice-president of The Center for Mindful Eating and as an adjunct professor in Portland State University's Interpersonal Neurology Certificate Program. He travels internationally, spreading seeds of mindfulness as a health and business consultant, keynote speaker, and mindfulness workshop leader. He lives in Portland, where he enjoys mindfully riding his motorcycle through Oregon's natural beauty. To learn more, visit mindfulpractices.com

DEDICATION

May suffering ones be suffering free,

May the fear struck fearless be,

May grieving ones shed all grief,

May all beings find relief.

May all benefits resulting from this book

serve as a drop in the ocean for all beings

on the dance to awakening and enlightenment.

ACKNOWLEDGMENTS

———◆———

This work has been touched by the many teachers, students, persons and spiritual friends I've encountered over the years. Special gratitude goes to the Venerable U. Silananda for his kind teachings on compassion, Randy Fitzgerald for his enthusiastic support, encouragement and creativity, and others who generously shared ideas that helped shape this book along the way. I am grateful for my friends and colleagues at PESI, particularly publisher Linda Jackson, whose passion for this book has carried through in many positive, artful, and creative ways.

I am grateful and indebted to my family, especially my mother Barbara, a deeply kind soul who must have been a spiritual guide in another lifetime, and who I am fortunate to have had as a guide in this one.

Finally, my creative and soul partner, Bak'u del cuore Maria, for helping make this book possible and for adding your unique touch, vision and ideas. Thank you for dancing with this book, and with me.

BOOKS BY DONALD ALTMAN

The Mindfulness Toolbox

Clearing Emotional Clutter

One-Minute Mindfulness

101 Mindful Ways to Build Resilience

The Mindfulness Code

Living Kindness

The Mindfulness Toolbox for Relationships

Art of the Inner Meal

Meal by Meal

Stay Mindful & Color

The Joy Compass

12-Weeks to Mindful Eating

Positively Mindful

A Course in Mindfulness

Contents

INTRODUCTION

———◆———

With all of life's chaos and distraction, it can be a challenge to focus and reflect inwardly. Possessing a human mind and body is an almost unimaginable gift. Yet at the same time it means that over time we are subject to fear and uncertainty. Distract or look away as you may, the body still ages and time still passes. Finances, jobs, health and relationships can shift direction in a moment, like the wind. How can we hope to make sense of this without being overwhelmed and saddened? But while all of this is part of human experience, the practice of reflection can help us to better understand and accept the nature and mystery of being.

Reflect follows the advice shared by the Buddha on his deathbed when asked how his teachings should be taught and carried onward. Instead of trying to codify his life's work, the Buddha simply said, "Be a lamp unto yourself." In other words, use your uniquely human capabilities, which are immense, to illumine and light your own path.

This book contains reflections designed to develop a penetrating awareness as they tap into what we often think as the mundane and ordinary, but which can simultaneously be experienced as the Sacred and Divine. The 6th century Italian monk St. Benedict, for example, wrote in his *Rules of St. Benedict* that monks should, "Regard all utensils and goods of the monastery as sacred vessels of the altar," because he believed there was no meaningless kitchen work. Reflection transforms the mundane into the sublime, and more.

Reflection caresses the light surfaces and dark shadows of the ego's confining I-dentity. It shines a laser-like beam of clarity on all our deeds, perceptions, and thoughts. It shatters old illusions and dualistic thinking, and allows for new mindsets while breaking the chains of past conditioning. It illuminates with surprising insights. It invites fresh ways of seeing and experiencing as it leads us into unexpected and untrodden pathways. It touches whatever we touch; even daily experiences with technology can be transformed when touched by reflection. This is the true seeker's path to reducing suffering, enhancing wisdom, and revealing secret treasures of the spirit.

Think of this book as a trusty companion, a touchstone to carry with you on your journey. You needn't follow these reflections in linear fashion.

Each topic, from nature and love to bliss and wisdom— are like facets of a diamond where any one topic reflects all the others.

Let's take a brief look at how each section in this book can help anyone to relieve suffering and access the wise voice within.

Simplicity & Peace contains reflections for slowing down, overcoming dis-traction, and embracing a more present-oriented approach to each day. You'll discover for example, how to easily use the breath to let go of worry and find greater stillness and calm.

Nature invites an enhanced awareness of the natural world. The reflections here open our eyes and hearts to the small, wondrous happenings all around—from morning's first light and nature's silence to capturing the meaning inherent in every new season.

Relationships is a section that can foster new hope, connections, and positive mindsets into your life. These reflections ask you to see the world and others through fresh eyes. These new perspectives hold the potential for deepening relationships of all kinds.

Love takes you on a journey toward exploring the life-changing riches available through the life-sustaining power of love and compassion. From going beyond cynicism to loving oneself, this section will inspire you to participate fully in your life.

Laughter reminds us that lightening up is an important means of coping with the challenges that life presents. Whether it's about learning how to break old toxic habits or take a more playful attitude toward your life, these reflections enhance joy—and bring a smile or two.

Bliss reveals how those most ordinary of moments are capable of bringing a sense of oneness, wholeness and joy. Instead of filling up, this section explores how to *fulfill* oneself—whether through savoring a single morsel or finding the contentment that is already at your side.

Transformation focuses on overcoming fear and worry about change. Here you'll reflect on how things—including the mind and body—are constantly changing and transforming. This awareness can remove limitations and liberate us so we can live more freely.

Wisdom demonstrates that by deepening our roots in the Here and Now, we become more attuned to all things. This inner knowing will help you tap the power of acceptance, gratitude, sharing your purpose, and other positive emotions necessary for wellness and harmony.

I like to think of this as a spiral journey with no beginning and no end. You might open to any page and see where it leads. Read these reflections more than once. Like a river flowing into the ocean, let them carry you to greater openness and spaciousness of heart, mind, and the eternal *Here and Now*.

simplicity
& peace

It's impossible to hold onto a river, but you can flow with it.

Feelings and thoughts are droplets
in an endless river
flowing out to the ocean.

None are final,
so why hold onto dissolving droplets?
Instead, watch them flow past and through.

This is nature's way,
and the way to find peace
with feelings and thoughts.

Reflect on this.

What is it like to observe—just for one minute—how quickly thoughts and feelings change?

How can noticing this flow be useful?

For one day, what is it like to be a keen observer of your thoughts, watching them pass by as fleeting and temporary visitors?

Be present with the next small thing, and then the next.

Make the in-between time count.
Notice all the little moments
of doing the dishes,
walking to the shower,
and hugging your partner.

This next simple moment
is where you get real-life traction.

Don't get lost in the future.
You'll get there anyway,
without even trying.

Reflect on this.

◎ What in-between moments do you neglect, ignore or push away?

◎ How could you be more present for the little in-between moments?

◎ How can you relish and remember today's ordinary moments?

**Embody each breath
as if it were your very last.**

How easy it is to forget
that each precious breath is
your lifeline with infinity
and a wake-up call to this moment.

Breath instinctively soothes, relaxes
and self-regulates.

Touch the breath's peace here, now.

Feel the moment rise and fall
like an ocean tide inside
as your breath goes in and out.
Ride the living wave.

Reflect on this.

⊚ For the next 60 seconds, ride the living wave of your breath from the tip of the nose all the way down to the belly and body.

⊚ What do you notice as you slow down and get present in this way?

⊚ When unfocused or overwhelmed, take 60 seconds to awaken to the embodied breath.

Do not be afraid of letting go of your worry.

Why live all clenched up,
holding onto fears and worries?

Let go of one worry
with this next out-breath.
Exhale naturally,
AHHhhh.
Now one more.

How lovely!

Reflect as you *AHHhhh.*

◎ What is it like to naturally let worry go with this next breath?

◎ What do you hold onto tightly that could be let go effortlessly, in this same way?

◎ What one worry could you release with the next out-breath?

Listen for the music of stillness, and you will be with peace.

What weapons of mass distraction
block you from the deep peace
of meditation, reflection
and repose?

Distractions of noise, busy-ness and technology
steal your peace like thieves in the night.

Serenity is much closer than you think.
Simply seek the music of silence
and find simplicity within.

Reflect on this.

How can you unplug and get more reflective?

How can you better tune into the music of the flowers, the earth, and the sky?

What one distraction can you remove or reduce today—in order to bring greater calm and simplicity into your day?

Everything in your life is already enough.

Step off the treadmill of unquenchable desire
where nothing is ever good enough.
Where envy and jealousy are thorny companions.

When you value and appreciate what is
already in your life,
you attain liberation from endless comparison
and negative emotions.

The joy of simplicity is right in front of you.
Let go of more, and find peace.

Reflect on this.

What is it like to be on the treadmill of wanting more, bigger, or faster?

How would it feel to live in "the what is" as opposed to "the what if"?

To overcome striving, what one thing can you value that is already in your life?

Every moment is both whole and empty.

No extra ingredients
or preparation is required.

Just mix and serve with bare awareness.
Experience the freedom that comes from
removing undue judgment,
mental confabulations,
and daily distortions.

Just awareness itself,
wide open like a flower.
Totally content as the flower it is.
Be the flower.

Reflect on this.

🌀 How do prior judgments and beliefs change how you experience each sensation, sight, sound, object?

🌀 What is it like to experience bare sensation and awareness itself?

🌀 For one day, how can you engage your child-like awareness and curiosity—seeing things as if for the first time?

Create an island of peace
at mealtime.

Eat calmly and you invite peace
into your body and mind.

But eat in anger and you will digest anger.

Each morsel is a blessing that can be savored
with deep appreciation and gratitude.
Surprisingly, even cheese dip.

Do this, one bite at a time.

Reflect on this.

◉ What effort—natural and man-made—went into the food you eat?

◉ How might a prayer, blessing, or silence change your relationship with your next bite?

◉ How can you create an island of peace at your next meal?

Cultivate a life journey
that leaves a sublime imprint.

What will your life imprint look like?
What sparkling glow will you leave behind?

The Universe knows
exactly how lightly or heavily
you tread upon the planet today.

Tread lightly and simply if you can.
Leave little behind,
except the warm glow of love,
compassion and peace.

Reflect on this.

◎ How gently and thoughtfully do you touch your world?

◎ How will your imprint affect future generations?

◎ What one small action can you make today—such as recycling—that will leave a lighter imprint?

It is only by disarming the ego that war truly ceases.

Some believe that fighting with others
is the path to peace.
Before you raise the sword against another,
see the truth of your own righteous love of war.

Without an ego,
who is around to look for a fight?

Only a mind of peace
creates more peace.

Reflect on this.

The next time you notice yourself being righteous, ask yourself what your ego gains by being so right.

What one bias or attachment can you hold onto less tightly, rigidly, or less personally?

Can you make a conscious decision to let go of the need to be right one time today? How does this feel?

nature

No morning (or moment)
is mundane.

So why sleepwalk through any morning?

Feel the poetry of dawn's fresh light.
Like a rainbow it splashes your day with color.
How will you greet it—as an honored guest
or ill-tempered servant?

Drink it all in.
Savor morning's soft music,
for this dawn will never come again.

Reflect on this.

◎ How do you greet mornings?

◎ What awareness could invite more poetry and wonder?

◎ Today, how can you deeply savor the ordinary yet special moments the morning offers? Then, carry one special morning experience with you today.

Tap the pure present by communing with nature in this moment.

Take nothing for granted.
Be faithful to all nature's bliss…
a light beam,
a bird,
a leaf,
air.

Bring your full attention to
Here and Now.
If you only remember one thing let it be this:
You must be present to participate!

Reflect on this.

If the great agricultural scientist George Washington Carver got his knowledge from "talking" to plants, why can't you?

Have you tuned in to nature's symphony today?

Today, spend a few moments outside in nature, tuning in to everything from the spacious sky to the ground. Is there something you feel connected with?

Nature plays a song that only the silent can hear.

Don't let your busy-ness get in the way.
If you really want to tune into nature's song,
you must first grow quiet.

Don't just *look* at a tree.

Peer deeply into its leafy green intelligence.
Feel its brown barky pulse.
Sense the Earth's entire wisdom
being drawn inward through sinewy roots.

Reflect on this.

When did you last recognize nature's elegant design?

What rhythms, objects, or sensations connect you to the natural world?

Start a daily practice of sitting in nature in silence. How does this help you tune into nature's song?

Your body is forever moving and dancing.

Your dance is a dynamic movement
between billions of cells.
A community dance, if you will.
Stop right now and behold the dance.

Notice the beating of your heart
as it pulsates in your palms and fingertips.
Hear and feel the natural choreography
of 20,000 daily breaths.

Even if you never notice,
you're always dancing to your own beat.
Find your own dance today!

Reflect on this.

⊚ How can you tune in to the body's dance?

⊚ What would it be like to express that dance outwardly with another, through a gesture, laugh, or hug?

⊚ How can you practice presencing and attending to the body throughout the day?

The experience of oneness
is not known through logic.

Nor can it be reduced into a formula.

Beyond thought and description,
awe and transcendence speak
in the language of mystery
grasped only by non-grasping.

Invite the darkly brilliant unknown
inside your own spirit,
for this is where wholeness lies.

From the mundane to the extraordinary,
there's nothing more to seek or look for.

Reflect on this.

🌀 In what ways did you discover wonder as a child?

🌀 How can you open your mind to the mystery of wholeness and oneness today?

🌀 Right now, surrender a pressing concern—releasing it to the Universe without expectation of a logical answer. How does it feel to open up in this way?

Every living thing
experiences seasons.

A tree naturally lets go of its leaves.
So why pretend
you don't have a fall and winter?

Yes, you can fight and resist aging with
fancy plastic surgeries and procedures.
Or you can honor and accept your seasons
with humility and grace.

Even winter's last, delicate melting snowflake.

Reflect on this.

◎ What is this season of your life, career, or relationship?

◎ Like a melting snowflake changes into water, how can each season in your life be accepted as a transformation?

◎ What can you honor about this current season in your life?

You are a *sense*-being not a *thought*-being.

So why be stuck in your head
with all those random, intrusive thoughts?

How many of today's thoughts tell you
something really profound about who you are?

Instead, drop into the body and come home.
Feel your feet on the floor.
Notice the brilliant colors around you.
Listen to the sound of your breath.
Taste your first food of the day.
Smell the sweet air.
Be a full sense-being today.

Reflect on this.

◉ How and where do you notice or bear witness to the body's natural sensations?

◉ When you lose awareness of those senses, how do you come back home?

◉ Breathe into your body's center—wherever you sense it, such as at the chest, abdomen, heart center, etc. How can you use this daily to invite greater ease, peace and balance?

To live authentically,
accept your true nature.

An acorn cannot grow into a palm tree
no matter how hard it tries.

Have others ever dictated that you become
a palm or an oak or a fir?
How would they know what seed lives within?

Become the seed you nurture.
How will you grow today?
What is your heart's path?

Reflect on this.

How will you make a difference in the world by being yourself?

What does it mean for you to choose your own life path?

What one thing can you do today to nurture your authentic self?

Everything changes and transforms, and then changes again.

From the body and consciousness
to raindrops and refuse,
nothing can avoid impermanence.

The next 60 seconds come and go
in the blink of an eye,
whether you do something or not.
So will the next 60 years.

This is not good or bad.
But it begs the questions:
What small thing can I do today to make a difference?
What one little thing can I share?

Reflect on this.

⊙ How can you be present or sit with an acceptance of the impermanent nature of life?

⊙ How does impermanence make this moment even more precious?

⊙ What small act—that you can do today—can make a difference?

relationships

There's a willing dance partner waiting for you.

Whoever says you can't dance
is mistaken.
Anyone becomes your graceful dance partner
when you move to her or his unique music.

Just take the next step forward.
There are no right or wrong moves
when you are being yourself.

And don't worry
about stepping on toes.
That's just part of the dance!

Reflect on this.

◎ Can you imagine another dancer's song?

◎ How could you join in with greater freedom and joy?

◎ How can you dance in step with the very next person you meet?

Don't take your next hello or goodbye for granted.

Be attentive when another arrives:
A touch, a smile, a kind word, a hug
makes one feel safe and included.

When leaving, choose a caring closure:
A hug, a kiss, or a wish for the day
sustains others on their journey.

Today, let each hello and goodbye
be an exercise in consideration,
filled to the brim with joy and kindness.

Reflect on this.

◎ What physical and emotional transitions do you experience with an important person in your life?

◎ What would it be like to stop whatever you're doing and be fully present during another's coming or going?

◎ Introduce one small, nourishing ritual to a relationship today. How could this change things?

When disappointment weighs you down, the helium of hope lifts you up.

Suffering is universal,
for everyone is subject to loss.
So yes, you can hold onto the heaviness and pain,
hurt and disappointment,
and no one will fault you for that.

Or, you can let your soul grow in appreciation
for all humankind in its frailty.

Find support and healing in the presence of others.
This is the nurturing way to fill your heart
with the helium of hope.

Reflect on this.

○ What old hurts, blames and disappointments do you carry on your shoulders?

○ What do you gain by holding on in this way?

○ What one hurt could you let go of just a little bit right now?

If you want to really communicate, first empty your cup.

Every opinion and belief you hold as
absolutely necessary is,
simply,
a singular and very human
way of looking at things.

Why do you insist on being so right?
What are you afraid of?

Empty your cup
and make space for new ideas.
How spacious!
Rest in the untangled moment.

Reflect on this.

How do your beliefs exclude others?

How can you let go of your assumptions—even for a few minutes?

Today, consciously "empty your cup" and deeply listen to one individual. What is this like for you and the other person?

If you want to extinguish joy, take things personally.

Almost anything taken personally
ignites your emotions
and snuffs out joy's light in an instant.

Look inward to untie this drama
that binds you up in knots.
When did it all begin?
How tightly wound is this knot?

Whatever it is,
the fire will only go out when you
stop throwing so much ego on it.

Reflect on this.

What things do you take personally that catch on fire?

How old is this emotional trigger, and how did it originate in your life?

Decide not to take an upsetting event personally today. How does this less reactive approach make you feel?

Each day presents an opportunity for new connections.

Get curious and let go of your assumptions.
Today, make a commitment to dialogue
with a heart of empathy and openness.
Seek to mutually explore truth with others.

When winning no longer matters,
you conquer the seeds of mistrust.

As the Buddha once said:
The winner sows hatred because the loser suffers.
Let go of winning and losing, and find joy.
This is how you build bridges of mutual connection.

Reflect on this.

◎ How could you drop your assumptions while talking with another today?

◎ How does letting go of an agenda change the feeling of a relationship?

◎ How does it feel to talk directly, honestly, and respectfully with one person today—without needing to win, be right, or prove a point?

Whoever graces your life
is here for a reason.

And if you're lucky,
you may even
figure out why
in this lifetime.

Of course, why wait that long?
Get to know others
without imposing expectations and needs.

Who is this one-of-a-kind,
most-unique-living-being
in-the-universe
manifested right before you?

Reflect on this.

Why do you think you are graced with the special persons in your life?

How does even that difficult person in your life have a purpose?

Today, refrain from imposing your expectations or needs on others. How does this let you experience others?

Everyone owns a big, messy can of worms.

When relationship problems repeat,
causing hurt, anger, and frustration, who's to blame?
Maybe no one.
Maybe it's just those two big cans of worms.

But before you blame the other person's worms,
look at your own worms first.
How do you keep feeding them,
keeping them plump and alive?

You don't need to fight or kill the worms.
Just take them out of your home
and put them back in the garden.
They'll be happier there, and so will you.

Reflect on this.

◎ What relationship "worms" follow you around?

◎ How can you move forward and still honor your past worms?

◎ How can you stop feeding your worms today?

If you live on this planet, it's not possible to escape trauma.

Yes, you could summon your trauma
until your last breath,
grabbing on for dear life and not letting go.

Or, you could start with a very different notion:
That every suffering being
in your proximity could benefit
from a kind deed, action, or prayer.

Say a blessing for your own
frail nakedness clothed in eternity.
What more (or less) could one possibly hope for?

Awaken on this!

⊙ Saint Teresa once asked the prisoners of San Quentin to pray for her. Who needs your prayers?

⊙ What would it be like not to define yourself by trauma?

⊙ Write down one blessing that could help you right now. How could this support you throughout the day?

Everyone has a
blind spot or two.

Most, if not every human on Earth
once believed it was okay to enslave others.
Does that make them any worse
or more ignorant than we all are?

Before you harshly judge others,
examine your own blind spots.

Judgment without wisdom is simply
another cruel slave-master.

Reflect on this.

⊙ How do you judge those with ideas different than your own?

⊙ How do these beliefs enslave yourself and others?

⊙ How can you use curiosity today to shine a light on your blind spot—as well as forgive yourself for the blind spot?

Befriend your own mind.

Yes, you can sit in the darkness,
watching the scary movie playing in your head.

Or, you can turn up the lights in the theatre,
and see you're really safe.

You're such a clever director creating that movie!
Now look around,
and step into the truth of the present moment.

Reflect on this.

○ How are things different when you stand back and observe negative and anxious thoughts, rather than grab onto them?

○ What's it like to step out of the movie theatre and into the Here and Now?

○ Today, think of one small way that you can assist your "director" in creating a different and more nurturing movie.

Each *Yes* is clearly defined by a *No*.

Everyone has the right to set boundaries
with the ultimate
veto power
of "no."

And sometimes, *hell no*.

It's okay to say "no" when it guards your safety,
self-care and well-being.
Without a *no*, a *yes* means nothing.

Reflect on this.

○ What "no" would you like to say to an employer, a family member, or a friend?

○ How can you say your "no" without a trace of anger or guilt?

○ List boundaries that benefit your physical, emotional and spiritual well-being. Today, how can you express just one of these?

The best way to get inspired is by inspiring others.

The next simple affirmation has the potential
to totally inspire and cultivate hope
in the one right before you,
as well as inside you.

What word, act or thought affirms you?
How can you share your hope?

Rest with this.

Reflect on this.

◎ When has a small affirmation or act of encouragement given you hope?

◎ How can you share that story with others?

◎ This day, offer one small act of kindness or goodwill to others at your workplace, home, or neighborhood.

Don't wait another moment to send the warm smile of love inward.

Since no one gets the perfect parent,
why not play the role of being
your own best parent and friend?

Acknowledge that you are doing your best.

Make time to pause,
inhaling the warm glow
of self-acceptance and self-appreciation.

Agree to make peace with whoever is in there.
Only then, can you make peace
with whoever is out there.

Reflect on this.

How can you befriend yourself in the next 24 hours?

How can you accept that you are doing your best?

Today, re-parent yourself in one kind and self-nurturing way. How could you do this again tomorrow?

You are not alone,
and you never will be.

Everyone is a point
on the infinite web of connectedness.

No one succeeds without the
support or guidance of others,
seen and unseen.

So when you feel alone,
shatter the illusion of separateness
by asking for what you need
and giving what you can.

See where you are on the web and reach out.
Even your thoughts connect you with others.

Blessings!

Reflect on this.

How could asking for help right this instant change your life?

Reflect on how everyone is interconnected.

Today, seek support from another. How does it feel to connect in this way?

To build winning relationships,
stop being addicted to winning.

Addiction to winning creates
an endless treadmill of duality:
Gain and loss,
fame and disrepute,
praise and blame,
pleasure and pain.

These worldly winds will forever blow
so long as you are attached to winning.

Instead, cooperate and co-win.
This way you sow seeds of
joy, happiness, and contentment
beyond winner and whiner!

Reflect on this.

How often do you compare yourself to others?

How in your life can you reach beyond winning and losing?

What one act of cooperation can you take with another today?

We link, therefore we co-are.

The Universe is co-relational
and co-creational.

To deeply gaze into someone's eyes
is to look back at yourself.

In the mirror of reciprocal recognition,
you each perceive and behold the other,
instantly and simultaneously.
Neurons interwoven across space.

That means that when you hurt another,
you inevitably harm yourself.

Awaken to this.

⊙ What quality of relationship have you co-created today?

⊙ How can you expand your we-thou awareness?

⊙ Today, how can you make another feel appreciated or
cared for?

There's a lot of fear
and negativity going around.

About how the world
is a scary and frightening place.

What you focus on becomes your world.
So use a simple blessing
of loving kindness to overcome fear.

Do this one little thing,
and you help make
the whole world safer.

Reflect on this.

⟳ What simple blessing for your health can you express in the next 10 seconds?

⟳ How could you make your blessings available to a loved one, friend, neighbor, stranger, unfriendly one, and even all persons and beings?

⟳ What blessing can you hold in your heart this whole day?

Kindness hides in plain sight.

Your kindness,
no matter how apparently insignificant,
makes every day a heart-filled journey.

Why hold onto your kindness?
Don't hide your smile,
your wonder,
your gifts.

Share your kindness and brighten the world.

Reflect on this.

◎ What does your kindness look like to others?

◎ How can you give time to another through kind listening?

◎ Offer one gift of kindness to another today. How can this become a daily practice?

Everyone gives up their secrets when you love them enough.

Only two simple things are required:
Full presence.
Full silence.

Empty your cup of the self,
for only then can you listen
with every compassionate
neuron, cell, and synapse
of your being.

Reflect on this.

◎ Do you dare to love with all your being?

◎ What would it be like to empty your cup of self?

◎ This day, share your full presence and silence with others.

Every loving deed and action you express returns as love.

If there were such a thing as an eternal law,
this would be it.

It has been said many times that
hatred does not extinguish hate;
only love is strong enough
to extinguish the flames of hate.

The secret is to trust enough to love
and love enough to trust.

Knowing this,
what's the most loving thing
you can do right now?

Reflect on this.

What does it mean for you to trust enough to love?

What would it be like to love without knowing or expecting what may come back to you?

Plant one small seed of love today.

When your heart gets cracked open like an egg, make an omelet.

If you have a heart, know it will be broken.
That's not the end of hope,
but the chance for a new beginning.

Let go of your expectations.
Sit with your broken heart.
Hold it. Comfort it.

And know that
love
is waiting around the corner.

Reflect on this.

☉ What happens when you get stuck in your hurt?

☉ How does your heart tell you it's okay to love again?

☉ What act of self-care can you nurture in your tender heart today?

Everyone you encounter today needs love and compassion.

So do you.

Yes, you can lead loudly with your hurt and pain.
(And gain some temporary attention
and some nurturing along the way.)

Or you can lead silently
with a quiet, compassionate heart…
…a heart open, tender, and soft,
and whose warm, persistent glow
comforts you and others,
without wanting.

Reflect on this.

How would leading with a compassionate heart change your life?

How would it change the lives of those around you?

Instead of complaining, bring compassion and understanding into your day's thoughts and actions. How does this change things?

The greatest riches are found in
your natural state of grace and awe.

The greatest poverty is living in anger and cynicism,
acting as if joy is simply an illusion.

Because everything matters.
Every ordinary and precious moment
holds the possibility for wonder.

Beyond the mind of cynicism
rests your innate, shining perfection.

It is here that your riches lie.

Reflect on this.

What would it be like to live with grace, beyond cynicism?

How would the cultivation of awe add to your life experience?

Today, set this intention: When cynicism arises let it go and open to the possibilities in this ordinary, precious moment. How marvelous!

Each cosmic particle is a precious giveaway of Divine presence.

The spark of life is the miracle
that infuses your very being with love.

Each expression of love you make
is the Divine spark shining through.

On your worst days,
Oh!
Sit with the awareness of how
blessed and loved you are!

Reflect on this.

◎ The Divine can be understood in many ways—as whatever is sacred, a blessing, or supremely lovely. Which expression of the Divine could be viewed as a miracle—such as sunshine, a bed to sleep on, clothes to wear?

◎ In what ways does your own Divine spark shine through?

◎ Today, choose something in your life—even something unwanted—which you can accept as a beautiful, mysterious gift.

What can you do, knowing that everyone will one day leave you?

Or you will leave them?
And no one knows when.

Yes, you can lament in fear,
be stricken with anxiety,
or, face the truth:
Precious moments you share with
another may never come again.

So why would you ever,
ever,
say hello or goodbye to someone
as if it didn't matter?

Reflect on this.

⊚ Knowing life is transitory and temporary, how can you make this moment count when with another?

⊚ What would change if this next hello and goodbye were your last?

⊚ Today, pay special attention to making each of your greetings/departures purposeful. How is this fulfilling?

You are never on the sidelines of life.

You are so totally in the game,
so why pretend you're not?

Don't wait *one more minute*
to share or encourage another.
As St. Francis advised,
For it is in giving that we receive.

Live your purpose today.
That is the game of being alive.
How one-derful!

Reflect on this.

◎ What is your special talent that makes you feel alive?

◎ What have you shared in the past, and how can you offer this to another?

◎ Today, make a point of encouraging someone or sharing something with another. How does this enliven a sense of purpose?

Every parent cares for their children
to the best of their inability.

Yes, you can complain
until the end of your days (and some do).
Or, you can embrace your childhood
in all its entirety.

Honor all the hurts and wrongs,
while appreciating all the
life lessons you were offered.

Now, consciously make an effort to do better.

Reflect on this.

How can you accept the limitations of your parents, and move on to get your needs met?

How can you accept your limitations and move on?

What is one valuable lesson from your childhood that you can utilize today?

Even the most hurtful person in your life deserves understanding.

Yes, you can deservedly remain upset,
vowing never to let go of this injustice.

But, if you remain locked
in your own prison of anger,
who is really suffering?

Only you can unlock the door.

Turn the key and step into the light.
Feel the warmth of acceptance
and peace that comes from letting it be.
The next small step is good enough.

Reflect on this.

How could you begin to forgive—or accept (not condone) what happened?

What would it be like to even imagine letting go of hurt and anger?

Write down one beneficial thing that might come from acceptance/forgiveness—today, or even one, five, or 10 years from now?

Look deeply into the roots
of your own dissatisfaction.

Yes, you may blame others for where you are.
But if you want to get unstuck,
you must first be open and present to
the part of this you own.

How much willfulness and non-acceptance
do you bring to this as-is moment?
How much mental energy do you put
into avoiding or loathing what you don't like?

No one else will do this for you.
Besides, things are not what they appear.
(Nor are they otherwise!)

Reflect on this.

◎ What small part of this moment—however disappointing or unwanted—can you embrace?

◎ How can you find even a little bit of acceptance for a difficult person in your life?

◎ For one day, make peace with one dissatisfaction or unwanted thing you deal with. How does this help you feel less constricted?

Your words, thoughts and intentions transmit a powerful vibration.

However subtle they may be,
your desires and intentions register to
the ends of the Universe.

Don't give the Universe a headache
by shouting your anger and unhappiness.

Whisper your deepest intentions for peace,
and you will spread seeds of
love and kindness to all beings.

Reflect on your intentions.

◎ How often do your words transmit peace, kindness, and understanding?

◎ How can you better tune in to the vibrations behind the words of others?

◎ Before acting or speaking, set intentions for peace, love, kindness and compassion as you move about your day. Journal your experience of intention-setting.

Outsource unsolvable problems to your Inner Infinite Intelligence.

Why look for an external guru to give you the answers
when you already possess a wise guide and guru within?

Focus on the breath,
be present, and open your heart.
Here is where your loving,
knowing, inner guru patiently awaits.

Don't force an answer.
Simply listen with all your presence.
The innerverse knows.

Reflect on this.

◎ What unsolvable and unlovable problems in your life can be outsourced?

◎ How can you access your inner guru, or wise, nurturing self?

◎ With this next breath (and next), what is it like to soften your heart and listen for the message from your wise self within?

Mother Earth gives freely.

All that you depend upon for survival—
air, warmth, food and love—
is a willing offering of Mother Earth.

Knowing this,
how can you thank Mother Earth for
such splendid and miraculous gifts?

Reflect on this.

⊙ What things in your life do you overlook and could you be grateful for?

⊙ How could you show Mother Earth your appreciation for these gifts?

⊙ How could you freely share a gift with others today?

Your body is like a living clay container.

It is caressed and shaped by every experience,
memory and emotion in your life.

It's also the ultimate amusement park ride.
And you never have to wait in line for a seat.

Take care of the body.
Respect and love it,
and it will give you
all that is required on your journey.

Reflect on this.

How does your body signal that you feel anger, sadness, anxiety, frustration, and other emotions?

When could you find the time to patiently sit with the body's presence and tune in to its needs for care and nurturing?

What one small deed shows respect for your body today?

laughter

Now and again life resembles a pizza.

The cheesier and messier it is,
the more we like the pizza.

Yes, a pizza brimming with "the works"
has more drama, sizzle, and flavor.
But if you're eating "the works" most days,
then maybe ask:

What makes me crave so much sizzle?

Would it kill me to try
a salad once in a while?

Munch on this.

☉ What toppings add drama and flavor to your "pizza"?

☉ Which ones are healthy, which are not?

☉ For this one day, how could you vary your emotional diet to find more calm and equanimity?

Goals are just momentary punctuation points on a bigger journey.

It's not just when you arrive that counts,
but *how* you get there.
If your goal-oriented perfectionist is pushing you,
simply smile back.

Remind yourself about
those in-between moments,
those moments along the way
that make any goal memorable.

The period at the end of the sentence
is no more important than the other letters.
It is only one character on your keyboard.
(And typos are sure to hippen.)

Reflect on this.

☺ How can you appreciate and tune in to the in-between moments?

☺ What might happen if you steeped yourself in the journey and worried less about the goal?

☺ How could you be more forgiving and kind to yourself as you move toward a goal?

☺ Today, release one outcome so that you can focus on the journey. What is an in-between moment you might enjoy?

Better to participate in the mystery than be slave-bound to the known.

The siren song of the safe and predictable
insulate from the unknowable
and the now-able.

Laughter and love bloom in the
creative space born of mystery and movement.
Don't get trapped in a straightjacket
of the safe and known.

The improvisation of a new day awaits.
Be the improv artist you are meant to be!

Improv on this.

What mystery engages your curiosity today?

What undiscovered beauty or potential for laughter have you unwrapped today?

How can you transform old habits today by viewing each unfolding moment as an improv?

Whether you wear Brand X, Y or Z, it's still Brand YOU.

There's nothing wrong with looking and smelling nice.
But if you're intent on hiding
outer and inner insecurities from others,
know this:
Everyone has insecurities.
And that's human.

Besides, exactly *who* or *what* feels better
by wearing Brand X, Y, Z?
Better to drop the worry,
and set free the laughing, naked one within.
Be an ego nudist.

Reflect on this.

What honestly makes you laugh, lighten up, and feel better about yourself?

If you removed all the Brands from your ego, what would remain?

What one thing could you take less seriously right now, today?

**No matter your age, you have
a child inside wanting to play.**

Is your child bound up in the chains of
adulthood, responsibility, and expectation?
How heavy those chains are!

Who warned you against removing these chains?
What purpose do they serve today?
If removed, how would your world fall apart?

Funny thing is:
No one else can remove the chains but you.
You hold the key.
Really, you do.

Reflect on this.

↺ Where is your joyful, curious child?

↺ When have you last communicated?

↺ Today, exercise your child power. How does this unchain your life?

Take the same path over and over, and you've got a heck of a rut.

Did you stop to think that
each step you take today—
in any direction—
creates a chosen path?

You better love your ruts.

But, if your ruts are keeping you stuck and miserable,
engage your intention, otherwise
known as your *free won't*—
your ability to pause and say "no" to an old behavior.

In this way, you consciously step
onto a purposeful path
of your own choosing.

How liberating!

Reflect on this.

☉ When can you next exercise your "free won't"?

☉ What does your next step tell you about your chosen path?

☉ Beginning today, what is one new healing and conscious path you could start creating?

A simple smile and a tender heart can change the world.

Each situation, however difficult,
can be greeted with understanding
and openness.

The next time another's suffering spills over onto you,
do your best to pause.
Forbear.

Smile inwardly with compassion.

Or better yet, buy a red clown's nose for them.
If that's not handy,
give them your real-life radiant,
all-purpose and all-warming
Smile!

Reflect on this.

What would it be like to smile, even just for the fun of it?

How do you feel when you get a kind smile from someone?

What would it be like to get an actual clown's nose to put on to lighten things up? We're talking seriously here! ☺

Today, what opportunities can you find to engage your smile with others?

Things get easier when you stop worrying about what others think.

Have you met any accurate mind readers?
And yet, we keep trying to read minds!

Yes, you can keep thinking about
the opinions and musings of others.
Or, you can learn to let it be,
a process which usually takes
a couple hundred years.

So, you might as well get started today.

Besides, chances are that others
are thinking about themselves.

Reflect on this.

What would change if you worried less about what others thought?

How can you tap into your own eternal mothering self?

Today, keep count of the number of times you catch yourself mind-reading. Then, unclench the mind and rest in the present. What's this process like for you?

Life is full of banana peels, but suffering after a slip is optional.

Each situation or burden has the potential
to (en)lighten you with laughter.

Why insist on crying each time
you slip on the banana peel of life?

Won't laughter do the job just as easily?
Your attitude in the face of the burdens
of pain, loss, or disappointment
is something you control.

Besides, another darn banana peel
is waiting just around the corner.

Reflect on this.

How often have you laughed today? What would change if you could laugh at your banana peels?

How can you start to lighten up?

What "banana peel" do you face that could you take less seriously today?

All that you fret over now will seem a lot less important in 5,000 years.

Yes, you care deeply about your life,
the world, the future generation, and the planet.

Does taking it seriously make you feel better?
More responsible?
More compassionate?
More determined and right?

Okay, all those things.
Do all those things you must do.

Then laugh.
You may as well,
because it's easier than crying.

Reflect on this.

🌀 Is your current worry really worth this much stress?

🌀 What does a broader perspective tell you?

🌀 In what area could you consciously choose to lighten up today?

bliss

Joy abounds mostly in the small nooks and crannies of life.

Find joy in ordinary moments, like:
Taking a step and feeling the body move.
Eating and digesting an apple.
Watching a hummingbird mid-flight.
Taking this next breath.

Yes, you can wait for some big, dramatic
accomplishment to punctuate your life.

Or, you can be receptive to the ordinary
and unforeseen joys right before you.

Reflect on this.

⊚ Reviewing the past week, what ordinary moments can you savor?

⊚ How can you more readily recognize ordinary moments that invite joy?

⊚ Today, find one ordinary thing that nourishes you with joy. How might you share this with others?

Body is the elegant integrator of
your inner-outer world experiences.

Bliss lives in each bodily sensation.

Grow silent and listen.
Feel each heartbeat
as it tingles in your fingertips.

Feel each breath
as it caresses the lungs.

See each vibrant image and color
as it glints in the eye.

Tap your personal inner-outer,
and know the bliss of Here and Now.

Reflect within the body.

Reflect on this.

How does your body mediate your inner and outer experiences?

How can you slow down enough to find peace and acceptance for whatever the body is sensing right now?

Today, tune in to the body's entire orchestra of experiences, movements and sensations. How does full embodiment change things for you?

There's a silver lining
in everything.

Yes, there are things you hate,
that disrupt your life and grate.
But how solid and permanent are these?

With each phenomena you witness,
there is also a silver lining
that materializes with the passage of time.

Soften, and look into your past,
and you will find the grace of silver linings.
It is the silver linings that
make life rich and meaningful.

Reflect on this.

⊚ What loss in your life has made the space for other doors to open for you?

⊚ What is an example from your life of something you initially thought was bad, but which turned out to have a positive consequence?

⊚ Today, what's it like to actively find a silver lining for a challenge that's occurring in your life right now?

You can only eat an apple one bite at a time.

Yes, you can try to gulp down an entire life in a day:
Be the most fit person in the gym,
work more hours than anyone else in the office,
be the most incredible partner, mom or dad,
and throw the most elaborate parties.

All of which will make you either amazing
or amazingly exhausted.

Why not slow down the pace
and savor life one little bite at a time?
Do this,
and you will not want for more.

Reflect on this.

How does running from one thing to another make you feel?

How could slowing down the pace help you be happier?

Right now, commit to one small change that will simplify your life each day. How and when can you put this into action?

Get off the happiness treadmill and find true peace in contentment.

You can climb on the happiness treadmill,
craving more and more like a hungry ghost
that can never be satisfied.

Or, you can cultivate contentment.

With its quiet inner sense of tranquility,
contentment is the knowing that everything is okay,
and that enough, really *is* enough.

Don't believe all the press releases about happiness.
Contentment may be quieter and less showy,
but it's a lasting and supportive companion.

Reflect on this.

What things promise happiness, but just leave you wanting for more?

What forms does contentment take in your life? What could it look like?

Today, how could you focus on contentment in a supportive way?

Use a beginner's mind to tap your constructive power.

Everyone suffers in some way from abuse of power.
If you have been an underdog
(and who hasn't),
don't let that be an excuse for
becoming just another cruel overdog.

Stop believing you have all the answers.

Start with a beginner's mind,
the spacious mind of *don't know*.
Seek answers with others,
mutually and with kind regard.

Do this, and neither a slave nor master be.

Reflect on this.

How can you begin to cultivate constructive power—such as by seeking input and ideas from others in your life and work?

How can being more open-minded help you to be more spontaneous and alive?

Today, intentionally cultivate "beginner's mind" in your interactions with others.

The most important person in your life is whoever is with you now.

Yes, you can pretend that you own or
purchase the future,
and that this moment is unimportant.

Or, you can be fully available,
ready to help the one
who is right before you
through the gift of understanding,
support and compassionate presence.

Is this not true bliss?

Remember, this moment is the most precious time.
For who knows when
you will ever see this person again?

Reflect on this.

◕ If you knew you would never again see the next person you are with, how would that change your level of forgiveness or understanding?

◕ How might this awareness alter your experiences with others?

◕ Today, bring a warm and tender openness to the next person you meet. How does it feel for you to be open in this way?

Don't hide from or be ashamed of your shadow.

Yes, you can deny the dark side,
seeing only what is safe and convenient.

Remember that light and shadow
are inseparable parts
of the same whole.

So bravely step into your dark unknown.

It is here that you will grow
in compassion for all parts of you.
How liberating!

Reflect on this.

How could you identify your own shadow?

Where and how does your shadow show up in your life?

Today, how could you invite your shadow into the light?

Better to be the oak tree you are than the palm tree you aren't.

If you really want to be miserable,
first compare yourself to others.
Then focus on what others have,
and what's missing from your life.

The oak tree wanting to be as skinny
as a palm tree is one very unhappy tree.

Be faithful to yourself.
Each tree is beautiful, unique.
Be true to yourself in order to
get free of envy, jealousy, and greed.
Such is joy and bliss.

Reflect on this.

How does comparison diminish or harm you?

How would it feel to appreciate yourself for what you've been given?

Right now, name one unique thing about you that you can accept. How can you cultivate greater acceptance?

Don't love your problems so much that they define you.

Every impossible puzzle
has an impossibly clever puzzle-maker.
If you strongly identify with your
difficult problems, you might even ask:
*Who would I be without all these important
problems?*

Peacefully accept and witness
the ego's need to be in charge.
For only then will you see
beyond ego, beyond mind, beyond suffering.

When nothing needs fixing—not even the ego—
all that's left is unbroken wholeness.

Reflect on this.

🌀 What role do you play in the puzzles/problems you have?

🌀 How often have you faced similar puzzles before?

🌀 Right now, how does it feel for you to contemplate letting go of the need to fix things in your life?

transformation

Accidents happen most when you don't pay attention.

It's easy to think that by some strange accident
you ended up with the life you have.
Somehow, this job or living situation just happened.

And when you weren't looking,
someone you adore (or don't) mysteriously climbed
into your bed for the last year or maybe 20.

Yes, you can live as if your life was an accident.

Or, you can pay attention to your intentions,
even those most subtle ones.
Do this, and you will be amazed
at who you are
and what you can create.

Reflect on this.

How can you start to notice habitual intentions that do not serve you?

When have you exercised your veto power over unhelpful intentions?

What is it like to set a conscious intention for every little thought, movement or action you take over the next three minutes?

Invite your unwanted emotions inside for a cup of tea.

Do you try to avoid negative emotions?
Yes, you can have your mental police
handcuff and put unwanted feelings
in a paddy wagon never to be seen again.

Or, you can invite them inside for a cup of tea.

What is the message behind the emotions?
Are you out of balance, needing rest,
needing safe boundaries, needing simplicity?

Before you call the police, have a cup of tea.
You may discover the supreme blessing
you've been waiting for.

Reflect on this.

How willing are you to invite unwanted emotions into your life?

What emotions would it help to invite in for a cup of tea and why?

Today, have a cup of tea with unwanted feelings. What new understanding is offered by doing this?

If you really, really want to bump into something, look backwards.

Turn off the static of the history channel.
Switch your remote to the clear reception
of the Here and Now.

Tune in to your feet on the floor,
your body sitting or standing,
your posture and the positioning
of your arms, knees, hands, shoulders.

One taste of this moment is enough.
The next time you're lost in the past or future,
take a taste of the Here and Now.

It's perfect just as it is,
and you don't need to change anything!

Reflect on this.

How often do you play the history channel?

When this happens, practice tuning in to the Here and Now channel.

For a five-minute span, stay in the Here and Now regardless of what you are doing. What did you learn from this practice?

A box is confining only when you never open it.

Most everyone once firmly believed
that the Sun
revolved around the Earth,
that the self
revolved around the ego,
and that truth
revolved around science.

The human mind constructs many kinds
of fixed mindsets and mental boxes.
Open your box and get free.

Reflect on this.

◎ What beliefs do you tightly hold onto as true?

◎ What keeps you from opening some of your "boxes"?

◎ Today, boldly step out of one of your long-held boxes. What do you notice?

Each door slammed in your face guides you toward beauty.

Why open the same slamming door
and expect a different result?

Slamming doors close for a reason.
Each is meant to guide you in a new direction.

Keep opening doors until you behold beauty.

When you step over the threshold
of a door meant especially just for you,
you become a life sculptor and artist of pure joy.

Reflect on this.

🌀 Which doors do you enter time and again, even if they do you harm?

🌀 What doors open willingly for you?

🌀 Today, what new door can you open in order to explore or learn more about?

Your awakened luminous nature is already beside and inside you.

Like an eagle dreaming it's a snake,
why crawl on your belly
when you can fly?

Your innate, awakened nature winks at you
to wake up to the eagle's eye view.
Open your senses wide and know
there is no other moment but this.

Let go of imagined limitations.
Fly!

Reflect on this.

What fears or worries keep you from flying?

If you could awaken to your full potential right now, how would that change your life?

Today, overcome one worry or fear in your life. What does it feel like to let go of this and fly?

Examine your attachments, and you will loosen old knots and patterns.

Those things belonging to the
I, me, my, and *mine*
reveal your attachments and clinging
to people, ideas, beliefs, objects.

Yes, you can hold tightly onto these,
relishing the sense of identity and control they offer.

Or, you can see the truth:
Clinging to what is fleeting and temporary
causes fear, pain, sorrow, loss and suffering.

Why wait another minute?
Loosen one small knot of attachment today.

Reflect on this.

How does the "I" "Me" "My" or "Mine" color your life?

What do you cling to or avoid that causes fear, worry and anxiety?

Right now, what one thing you feel is a "necessity" in your life could be viewed simply as a "preference" instead?

There is a place where things just are.

Imagine discovering a special place
where everything you experience
is free from judgment.

Everything just *is*.
Perfect as it is.
Abiding as it is.

No mental additions or subtractions
will ever make this place any better or worse.
This special place exists within you.

Boundless, choiceless awareness is your birthright.
You were born with it!

Reflect on this.

◎ What would it be like to witness things just as they are?

◎ How does your mind act as a mental filter that dramatically changes how you view daily events and experiences?

◎ Right now, what is it like to open your entire being to the "what is" one minute at a time?

Impermanence is permanent;
uncertainty is certain.

Without change, the child could
never grow into a beautiful young adult.
Without change, there could be no
transition from summer to fall to winter to spring.

You can choose to fight, reject and fear change.
Or you can let the light of acceptance
shine on your own neighborhood,
in your own body,
in your relationships and your career.

Change is forever, and fears are temporary too.
How sublime!

Reflect on this.

How can acceptance help you step back from the fear and worry of change?

What do you fear most about change?

What one change could you accept more starting today?

**Every gourmet meal
leaves behind a dirty mess.**

Why be surprised when life gets messy?

Instead of eliminating the mess,
embrace and accept
this perfectly imperfect meal that
Chef Karma has prepared specially for you.

After all, didn't you bring the ingredients?

Reflect on this.

How could you appreciate the messiness that is life?

How could acceptance help you to live with difficulties—such as an illness, loss of a loved one, or a change in circumstance?

For a day, what perfectly imperfect part of your life could you be okay with?

To truly change your life,
you must first focus your mind.

Are your intentions beneficial to yourself and others?
Are they really *your* intentions,
or have they been hijacked by others?

Don't take your intentions and thoughts lightly.
First silence your digital masters.
Next, do a daily brain workout by counting
each breath you take up to 10, then 25, then 50.

The brain is a quantum environment where
each focused intention rewires the brain.
This literally changes how you will think in the future.
How empowering!

Reflect on this.

What have you already materialized in your life?

What intention(s) can lead you to manifest your dreams?

Today, do the brain workout described. How might you continue this practice?

Live in the *what is*,
not the *what if*.

Have the courage to face life as it is.
Notice what you are attracted to,
what repulses you,
and what you are indifferent to.

Yes, you can act impulsively and reactively,
or you can step back and pay attention.

What's really happening here?
Just sit without needing to respond,
and you will see more clearly and get free.

Reflect on the *what is*.

◎ Do you more often live in the "what is" or in the "what if"?

◎ What's it like to sit with the truth of the moment instead of avoiding it?

◎ Get curious about the times you struggle to face life as it is.

Death is just another word for transformation.

Most, if not everyone wonders:
What is death?
What will come after?
Will there just be the void of nothing?

As Einstein said:
Energy cannot be created or destroyed,
it can only be changed from one form to another.

Everything and everyone
is in a process of becoming.
Besides, life is for the living,
so make the most of it,
and live!

Reflect on this.

◎ How does the question "What is death?" affect your life?

◎ How does it help or hinder to dwell on it?

◎ Right now, can you release the unknown future, so as to contact the freshly arising Here and Now?

The true felt-sense of this moment cannot fully be known using only words.

During upsetting events, you can stick to
the old story of
"I am depressed/anxious/sad,"
and distance from the real feelings.

Or, you can dive into the felt-sense of Here and Now,
noticing the heaviness, the uncomfortable,
the unwanted,
the lightness, the uplifting, the pleasantness,
or the something in-between.
See how these constantly shift like the wind.

In this way, even upsetting memories or events
are like clouds that arise in the moment
and then fade away.
Would you grab onto a cloud?

Reflect on this.

⊚ What old story seems to repeat in your life?

⊚ How has grabbing onto old stories helped or hindered you?

⊚ When a repetitive or upsetting story surfaces in the mind, shift your awareness to the felt-sense of the body—so you experience it freshly, beyond the limitation of words. Give yourself time for this practice.

Most, if not everyone
I-dolizes the I-dentity.

Oh cult of *I*, how *I* adore *I*.
I couldn't live without *I*.

Like the Wizard of Oz, the *I* pretends to be in charge.
It divides one-ness into little, confusing pieces
of good, bad, right, wrong.

Right now, ask:
Where is the voice in my head that sounds like me?
Who is doing the listening?

Even recognizing the *Wizard of I* just as is
and without having to push it away,
is to discover wholeness.

Reflect on this.

⊙ What is your favorite I-dentity story at this moment?

⊙ What would it be like if you held onto this a little less tightly?

⊙ For one day, release your favorite I-dentity story. How does this change things?

Speak and step lightly and purposefully, leaving few tracks.

What do today's choices say about you?

Yes, you can disregard others,
littering the environment with
thoughtless words, deeds and actions.

Or, you can live your life on purpose,
inviting sensitivity and compassion
into each and every choice.

Walk gently and peacefully,
and you will inspire others
to follow in your footsteps.

Reflect on this.

⊙ How could you more compassionately move about your day?

⊙ What purposeful "steps" have you taken recently?

⊙ For the next day, how can you show consideration and sensitivity for your environment?

The mind is like a wild mustang that will kick you unless trained.

Everyone owns a mind that is infinitely
more stubborn and willful than the wildest mustang.

Don't give up.
Train your mind through discipline,
consistent effort, diligent practice,
and a nice fat carrot or two.

Each day, saddle up by watching the breath,
noticing even subtle thoughts and emotions,
and experiencing the felt-sense of life.

Do this, and your mustang will be in your service,
instead of the other way around.

Reflect on this.

◎ Where does your wild horse tend to run during the day?

◎ How can you start to tame your wild horse?

◎ What discipline can you bring to taming your wild horse today?

wisdom

Be grateful for the little things,
and you'll never be disappointed.

Swallowing a bite of food,
taking a step,
turning your head,
singing out loud,
taking a breath.

If you could not do these simple things
life would be suffering,
if not impossible.

Look around and find the little things,
from A to Z.
How fortunate!

Reflect on this.

◎ Which miracles have you noticed today?

◎ What miracles surround and bless you at this very instant?

◎ Today, share with another person one thing you are grateful for, plus tell why you are grateful for this.

Stay true to your values, and you'll become the person you want to be.

There's nothing separating you from the likes of
Gandhi,
Martin Luther King,
and Saint Teresa.

They followed their values one day at a time,
with disciplined determination,
to create an intention-driven life.

Do you truly want to be kind,
respectful, compassionate?
Do not think it impossible.

Take one step towards
the person you want to be today,
and then do it again tomorrow.

Reflect on this.

◎ Who is your personal hero and why?

◎ What values define this hero?

◎ For this day, how can you embrace one value that matters?

If you only do one thing,
light another's candle.

There are so many ways to be a light giver.

When you light the way
as a mentor, a helper, a volunteer
or even an anonymous giver,
you spread the light of hope.

Reflect on the light givers
in your own life.
Feel the warmth of that glow,
even years later.

How wonderful to light a candle!
Light one today.

Reflect on this.

◎ What would it mean for you to light another's candle?

◎ Who did this for you in your own life?

◎ Set the intention to light another's candle today. How does it feel to help another flourish?

Look deeply and penetrate the deeper connectedness of all things.

Just as a table was once a tree,
so is your car a composite of other things.
No-thing is as it seems.

Even the atoms of air we breathe
have likely been touched by the dinosaurs,
Jesus, Muhammad, and the Buddha.

All that is, began as something else.
Even the Cosmos was once compressed
to the size of a pinhead.

Use your penetrating awareness to sense
beyond the beyond.

Reflect on this.

◎ How could you start to sharpen your penetrating awareness?

◎ What one positive thing changes by your recognition of connectedness?

◎ Today, notice even the slightest moments of bare awareness, when you are freed from the thinking and commenting mind.

If you live on Earth, then you are subject to extreme wear.

This means that everything—
from new tires to the most gorgeous people—
will experience a few wrinkles
and occasional baldness.

That's not all bad.

It's just all the more reason for you to
take good care of this body (or car).
Even though both
will get recycled.

Reflect on this.

How ready are you to live with your own body's wear and tear?

How can you view life's wear and tear with greater acceptance?

Today, what is one way you can strive to keep your body and mind healthy?

Find lasting joy not in temporary cravings, but in the eternal now.

Craving external objects
may bring temporary pleasure.
But what was once a novelty
soon becomes tired and tiresome.

The eternal now is always fresh,
always abundant,
always sublime,
always profound.

It is also free.
And no monthly subscriptions are required.

Reflect on this.

What helps you cross over the river of ceaseless craving towards joy?

What gets you most into the present moment?

Today, whenever you're lost in thoughts, simply come back to your senses to cultivate in-body Here and Now awareness.

Every challenge offers an opportunity for cultivating wise presence.

Each frustrating moment spent waiting in line
can be used to grow patience and surrender.
If this idea makes you angry,
go stand in the longest line you can find.

Whether facing the good, the bad, or the indifferent,
wise presence simply asks that you pause
and observe with child-like curiosity.

Now, take a breath, and inquire:
What does my wise presence ask of me?
What potential exists in this Here and Now
waiting to blossom forth?

Reflect on this.

What expectations and "shoulds" provoke your impatience?

What would it be like to untie the knot of harmful emotions by pausing and observing them?

Today, embrace your wise presence and patience when faced with an obstacle. How does this assist you?

If you really want freedom from suffering, look at what you cling to.

Is there the memory of lost love that you hold onto?
Is there an idea you are stubbornly attached to?
Is there an expectation you refuse to let go of?

Yes, you can remain in pain,
reliving that horrifying loss and trauma.

Or, you can recognize that it's not the loss,
but the *clinging* to the loss
that causes suffering.

If it helps, always know that
you are not alone in your sorrow.

Reflect on this.

⊙ How can the universality of loss help you have compassion for all—including yourself?

⊙ How does grasping or attaching to anything cause additional suffering?

⊙ Today, how can you share a loss as a way to release it?

Everyone possesses a miraculous healing instrument.

And it isn't necessarily your doctor.

Your body is a sublime instrument
of harmony and healing
developed over tens of thousands of years.

Visualize the body as healthy and in complete balance
as it was designed and intended to be.
Send it your inner intention for healing.
Let each in-breath fill it
with lightness and well-being.
Exhale out the impurities.

In this way, rest in wellness and harmony.

Reflect on this.

Did you ever have to try to heal a cut, or did your body know what to do?

How can you practice intention to support your innate healing powers?

Reflect on how your intention to heal has aided you in the past, and how it can help you right now.

To stay present, invite the right friends into your life.

Just as the flu spreads by close contact,
an emotional illness spreads
by exposure to the poisons
of jealousy, envy and ignorance.

While you will encounter all kinds
of persons in your life,
you need to find persons who
protect and support your Here and Now practice.

Seek out ways to practice wise presence with others.
This will sustain you in difficult times.

Reflect on this.

◎ If you were being brutally honest, who brings negativity into your life?

◎ How could you buffer yourself from this negativity?

◎ Today, how could you cultivate friendships with others who are practicing Here and Now awareness, also known as presencing?

Safeguard your awareness as you would a most precious treasure.

Imagine two museums filled with priceless artifacts.
One is unattended and unlocked;
the other is both guarded and locked.
Which treasure is more likely to get robbed?

Desires, alcohol, and addictions
are just a few of the things that
will steal away your awareness,
causing harm to yourself or others.

Start by noticing those moments
when you lose awareness of your awareness.
In this way, you practice presence.
Protect your treasure.

Reflect on this.

What steals away your awareness that is harmful or dangerous?

How have such "thefts" affected your life and choices?

While no one can be aware all the time (and that's ok), how can you best guard and protect your presence today?

Everyone deserves dignity and respect.

Humankind is a work in progress,
dynamic, learning and growing.
Give space and understanding to others.

Yes, you can shout in someone's face
that they are ignorant and insensitive
and disrespectful.

Or, you can be the gentle breeze that carries
seeds of dignity and respect.
Let your soft, persistent voice be like
water carving new pathways
of understanding, courtesy and kindness.

Reflect on this.

What would it be like to disarm and reduce your own insensitivity?

How can you bring a soft voice of understanding to heal suffering?

What one thing could you do in your own neighborhood, right now, as a way to start spreading dignity and respect?

When tempted to fix others' gardens, pull your own weeds first.

It's easy to judge others,
seeing them simplistically
in black and white.

Who would you rather have as a neighbor?
A kind meat eater like the Buddha,
or a cruel vegetarian like Hitler?
No one is defined by a single opinion or behavior.

Better to see others in three dimensions.
Then, pull your own weeds so as to cultivate
a welcoming garden of kindness and peace.
Let your example water the gardens of others.

Reflect on this.

What are some of your own weeds, or biases, that could be pulled?

Which side of a polarity are you unable or unwilling to see?

Right now, how could you water your garden of openness and peace?

Every life challenge contains seeds of its own soul-ution.

Awareness is a spiritual path that harkens
the spaciousness within.

Enter this spacious, creative space
and you may discover that an
elegant soul-ution awaits you.

Inquire deeply:
What is the lesson to be learned from this challenge?
What if this challenge were not viewed in terms
of "good" or "bad"?
How could I grow personally
and spiritually from this challenge?

Reflect on your soul-ution.

◎ What challenge in your life could benefit from a soul-ution?

◎ How might you grow from this situation?

◎ Today, what is it like to rest in spaciousness, without any expectation of getting a result?

Stop watching the clock, and wade in the pool of the timeless now.

Present-moment awareness is void of
conventional time.
The timeless Here and Now is your personal pool,
waiting for you to jump in
and take a refreshing swim.

Right now, stop. Look around.
Be present with your surroundings,
your body,
your breath,
all your senses,
and the conscious mind.
Awareness itself.

You can always enter the pool of endless,
timeless Now.

Reflect on this.

When have you been in the flow, even losing track of time?

What would it be like for you to stop watching the clock?

For the next three minutes, take a swim in the Here and Now, regardless of what you are doing or how overscheduled you might be. How can you swim like this more frequently?

You are a physical, mental, emotional, spiritual being, living as one.

We have been told we are a composite of parts:
Doctors care for the body.
Ministers care for the spirit.
Psychologists care for the emotions.
Educators care for the mind, and so on.

But that's an illusion.
You inhabit all these places at once
as a whole-istic being.

Find equanimity not just in the mind.
Express love not just from the heart.
Touch the Divine not just from the spirit.
Live as one being, undivided.
This is your human birthright.

Reflect on this.

○ What does it mean to view yourself as a whole-istic being?

○ How could this broader perspective be integrated into your life?

○ Right now, imagine taking a whole-istic viewpoint of a current life issue or concern. How does this transform your understanding?

Doubt is a good place from which to find wisdom and strength.

Don't be afraid to question your awakening practice.
Be willing to re-examine your values and ethics.

Use your doubt to help you learn more.
Seek out wise counsel,
knowing that skepticism is a path
toward greater knowledge.

Doubt is a not a weakness or sign of failure.
Use it to focus on how to improve your practice.
Instead of being grounded by doubt,
let it wake up your inner doubting St. Thomas!

Doubt on this.

☺ How can your doubt be a teacher?

☺ What emotions or beliefs hold your doubt in place?

☺ Think of one way that an obstacle or doubt can help
you learn more about your practice.

The Universe is an origami, and you are a master enfolder of awakening.

If humans possess potential for awakening,
then this potential can only exist because we are
the natural by-product of an awakened
planet and Cosmos.
Is that so hard to believe?

That essence of awakening is already enfolded in
your cells, genes, life and being.
Some call this Buddha Nature,
Christ Consciousness,
Integral Living,
Oneness.

Just as babies innately know to walk,
the power of Here and Now exists within.

Awaken on this.

🌀 How can you bring greater awareness to your natural spacious mind?

🌀 What tends to get you stuck in the narrow "I-me-my-mine" view?

🌀 What is it like to accept your awakening practice just as it is right now? How can you invite inner kindness as you stay on the path?